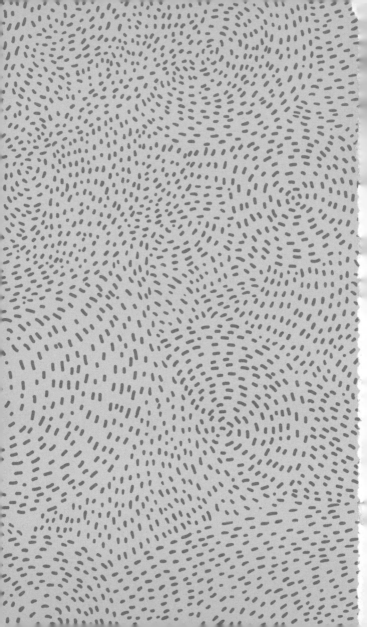

_____

TO

_____

FROM

_____

DATE

BRIGHTER
DAYS
AHEAD

50 Devotions of Hope in the Hard

Written by: Janice Thompson
Cover Design by: Becca Barnett

Printed in China
Prime: J6790
ISBN: 978-1-64870-292-1

CONTENTS

INTRODUCTION

Life is hard. (Can I get a witness?) We live through ridiculously difficult seasons. And we walk through valleys so deep that we might begin to doubt that sunshine even exists. We might even start to believe that we were meant to stay in the pit. But deep down, we think surely we were made for more than this; surely we were made for the radiance of the overhead sun on our cheeks and the balmy breeze wafting through our hair. Are you there? Are you ready to rediscover the possibilities of a bright future, one where you not only survive the tough seasons but actually thrive?

These fifty devotions were written with you in mind, not for those blissful seasons when you're soaring from mountaintop to mountaintop but for those icky times when nothing makes any sense. When you want to give up.

May you be reminded through these verses, affirmations, and quotes that you're not in this alone. God is as near as your next breath, and He's ready to fill you with hope for the future. That's what you need right now, isn't it? Hope is the great energizer, the life-giving force that can pull you up by your bootstraps and set your feet on a path toward a bright tomorrow.

There really are brighter days ahead. Oh, I know . . . it might not seem like that right now as you're trudging through the muck and the mire, but beyond these present circumstances there are happy tomorrows. Don't ever give up on the notion that you can find beauty in the midst of the ashes. It's there, calling your name, even now.

Don't give up on the cusp of what could be a breakthrough. Allow God's presence to guard your heart, even in the middle of the pain. And let the glimmers of sunshine peeking through the clouds remind you that rough patches—even the insanely hard ones—don't last forever.

YOU'RE NOT ALONE

You're imperfect, and you're wired for struggle,
but you are worthy of love and belonging.

Brené Brown

L ife is messy. The struggles are real and can
be a punch in the gut at times. There are
days when you wish you could stay in bed
with the covers pulled over your head. (Please,
Lord?) Well-meaning friends try to coax you
back to the sunlight, but all you can see is the
rain, so you resign yourself to the notion that
things are never going to get better. (Boo! Hiss!)

Then—gasp!—you realize you're not alone.
Seated in the cubicle next to you at work is
a gal who just lost her husband. You can see
the heartache resonating in her tear-filled eyes.
And, in another cubicle not far away, an elderly
coworker has just received a cancer diagnosis.
The weariness in her voice cuts to the heart.

You squint to see your boss as he passes
through the room. He's on his cell phone, angry with someone on the other end of the line.
He ends the call with an exaggerated groan.

Would hollering, "Been there, done that!" be
inappropriate?

Your thoughts begin to shift. On some weird
level, knowing you're not the only one struggling helps.

You rise and take a few steps toward the friend dealing with the cancer diagnosis. Her slumped shoulders reflect the weight of what she's carrying. Her red-rimmed eyes are puffy. You take a seat next to her and whisper, "You're not going to go through this alone, I promise." She takes your hand and gives it a squeeze, then glances your way with a glimmer of hope in her eyes.

As you make your way back to your seat, the Lord echoes those same words back to your heart: "You're going to make it through this. The answers might not come today. They might not come tomorrow. But you are wired for this and things will eventually get better. There are brighter days ahead. No, really."

AFFIRMATION

I'm wired for this.

SHIMMERS OF LIGHT

I will love the light for it shows me the way, yet I will
endure the darkness for it shows me the stars.*

Og Mandino

You've done all the right things. Truth be told, you've gone above and beyond. But the situation still isn't resolving. In fact, it's getting worse by the moment. Ugh. Well-meaning friends spout the old adage "When you reach the end of your rope, tie a knot and hang on!" but you want to slug them. (Would that be wrong?) Right now, you're too exhausted to remember how to tie a knot, thank you very much. Don't they get that? And do they really think sugar-coated platitudes will help?

These impossible situations spin into your life like unexpected meteors and threaten to take you down. Let's face it, life is hard to manage once your hope is zapped. But God wants to remind you today that He's in the hope business. There are shimmers of light, even in the darkest situations. If you look for them, you will surely find them. And when you do, those little hope beacons can change everything.

Kendra experienced this firsthand. When her daughter Jenna was hospitalized for nearly a month with cystic fibrosis, Kendra nearly lost her ability to hang on. Between her job, the daily trips back and forth to the hospital, and plenty of chaos from her other three kids, hope nearly slipped out the window. But then, in the middle of the struggle, something rather miraculous occurred. Jenna made friends with another girl she shared a hospital room with. In fact, the two became so close that Jenna cried on the day she had to leave the hospital. They vowed to remain close, to never lose touch. And they kept that promise.

They are teensy-tiny things, these shimmers, but they are mammoth when you glance in the rearview mirror years later. Little beacons of light bring hope and whisper, "Hang on! Don't give up!" They shift your focus upward, away from the situation and toward the One who is big enough to manage it.

What impossible circumstances are you facing today? Look up! Stars are twinkling overhead, begging you to remember that hope can still be found, even in the impossible.

AFFIRMATION

Even in the dark, I will look for
shimmers of light.

---

*Og Mandino, The Greatest Secret in the World (New York: Bantam Books, 1978), 22.

WHEN LIFE GIVES YOU LEMONS

Start by doing what's necessary;
then do what's possible; and suddenly
you are doing the impossible.

Francis of Assisi

You didn't ask for it. You certainly don't deserve it. And you're most assuredly not feeling up to making lemonade out of it. But life has given you another lemon to add to the ever-growing pile, and you'd like to give it a swift kick back to where it came from. You're done. Finished. Kaput. One unfair circumstance after another has tried to knock your knees out from under you. You're beginning to wonder if there's some sort of target on your forehead. There's certainly one on your heart. These things you're facing are unjust. They're downright cruel, in fact.

You've moaned. You've groaned. You've turned multiplied choruses of "Why me, Lord?" into your swan song, and you're now ready to give a final encore. But those sour lemons keep flying your way as more inequities come. They pile up around your feet at the office as you face ongoing issues with your boss. (Really? You're accusing me of not doing my fair share? I work harder than anyone else here!) They seem to pelt you when the kids get home from school. (Are these kids of mine going to hate each other forever?) And they threaten to drown you when you attempt to pay the bills. (More month than money . . . again?) How is any of this fair?

It's easy to grow bitter when life is unjust. But there's something to be said for that old expression about turning lemons into lemonade. You can't control the unfair. But, with God's help, you can sweeten the taste by inviting Him into the situation. You might not notice the change in taste right away, but if you'll shift your perspective even a little, He might just surprise you with a tiny sip of goodness, right there in the middle of your pain.

AFFIRMATION

Life doesn't have to be fair to be full.

NUMB

By default, most of us have taken the dare to simply survive. Exist. Get through. For the most part, we live numb to life—we've grown weary and apathetic and jaded . . . and wounded.

Ann Voskamp

"How are you feeling about all of this?"

Megan shrugged in response to her best friend's question. How could she possibly put into words what she was feeling? Or not feeling, as the case might be. After all she'd been through over the past several months, the idea of allowing herself to feel seemed like too much.

Megan paused and then let out a sigh: "I think I've lost the ability to feel. I'm just . . . numb. And that's going to have to be okay right now. It's all I can manage."

Maybe you can relate. You've been so inundated by the onslaught of attacks that you've constructed massive brick walls to keep out the pain, carefully jabbing mortar into any cracks. You hope and pray those walls will protect your heart, but you can't deny the obvious: they've also totally blocked out any emotions that might have penetrated the surface and offered some sense of relief. You can't cry. You can't laugh. You can't seem to do much of anything . . . and you've reconciled yourself to that fact. But deep down inside you wonder if things will always be this way.

Let's face it—Novocain is great when you're seated in the dentist's chair, about to undergo a root canal, but it's only meant to be temporary, until the worst of the pain passes. If your mouth remained numb forever you would have a hard time functioning.

The same is true with your heart. Numb is okay for today. But what happens when we invite the numbness to stick around for weeks, months, or maybe even years? How long should we let it drag on? Could it be that we actually need those feelings in order to survive? Maybe it's time to ask God if there is a reason for the painful feelings. Ask Him to return them to you. Today might be a good day to take a risk—and ask, knowing that the One who answers will walk with you through it all.

AFFIRMATION

Today I will dare to feel.

FULLY FULL

My brokenness is a better bridge for people than
my pretend wholeness ever was.

Sheila Walsh

Picture a bicycle. You've ordered it from an online store and it just arrived at your front door, but it's missing something—the handlebars. Weird.

Imagine a cake. The baker added all the ingredients except one—baking soda. Instead of receiving a light, fluffy concoction, you're presented with a solid lump of baked flour. Ick.

Now envision a brand-new car on the showroom floor. It's ready to go, except that it's only got three wheels. Um, no thank you.

These might seem like odd illustrations, but this is how we view ourselves at times. We feel incomplete, as if we're not enough. We're missing tires. Or handlebars. Or baking soda. And we go through life wondering if we'll ever find the missing parts so that we can feel fully baked (er, whole). It's hard to live a full life when your glass is half-empty, after all.

Oh, but listen! Today, the Lord is whispering to your heart: "You are enough." Allow those words to sink in as you analyze their meaning: "You don't have to do anything or be anything more than what you already are." Your loving heavenly Father finds great value and worth in you, not because of anything you've done but simply because you're His child. And He wants you to begin to see yourself that way too. Instead of focusing on the missing parts, accept the love that He's offering you, just as you are.

You might be broken. You might be a hot, half-baked mess. But He sees you as beautifully whole and fully full. So, don't miss out on one moment of life or waste too much time looking to complete yourself. In Him, you already are. And boy, does He have amazing plans for all your tomorrows! So hang in there, sister! There are brighter days ahead.

AFFIRMATION

I'm fully full and more
than enough in Him.

INSIDE YOUR STORY

Rivers know this: there is no hurry.
We shall get there some day.

A. A. Milne

When an author sits down to write a novel, she creates an exciting cast of characters and gives them a plot filled with breathtaking twists and turns. There are mountain peaks and valleys deep. She creates the perfect setting, one that makes sense to both story and cast. And she somehow merges it all into one lovely tale that keeps you turning page after page.

Each character has a backstory, of course. Those "who he used to be" bits offer the reader bread crumbs . . . clues, if you will. If you know where someone has come from, it's easier to see where he is and where he's going, after all.

Still, if you pay close attention, you'll notice that a good author doesn't dump all the character's backstory in right away. Tiny snippets of it come out as the plot moves along. This is what keeps you, the reader, interested in turning the pages—all is not revealed at once.

You have a backstory too. You've been through a lot. And God (who happens to be an amazing Author, by the way) isn't spending a lot of time throwing your backstory into your present situation. He's also not throwing it in your face. Sure, it had some fascinating plot points. Yes, it has made you into the person you are. There's no denying some of the places you've been or things you've done. But He is more concerned with today. And tomorrow.

Maybe you're worried about what other people think about you, based on where you've come from. Remember: they've come from someplace too. And just because you can't see their backstory doesn't mean it's not there. Every person on Planet Earth wishes he or she could change certain elements of the past. (If only!) But there's a reason it's called backstory. It's behind you now. And it's mighty hard to go forward if you keep looking back.

That's what the Lord wants for you, by the way—forward motion. Stepping into a bright future. Trusting Him, in spite of the backstory.

AFFIRMATION

I will not allow my past to define my present or my future.

THOSE BEAUTIFUL UGLY TEARS

*A diamond is a chunk of coal that
did well under pressure.*

Henry Kissinger

If you ever want to give yourself a shock, take a peek in the mirror when you're in the middle of a good cry. Ack! Who is that woman staring back at you, the one with the mascara running down her cheeks? The one with her lips tugged down in a frown? You don't recognize her at all! Of course, the puffy eyes aren't helping. They've affected your vision. You can barely see the reflection staring back at you, can you?

Becca did her best to avoid the emotions bottled up inside her as she fought the temptation to cry. The season she found herself in had tossed one heartbreak after another her way. She just couldn't seem to catch a break. But releasing the pain? Letting the tears out? She wasn't sure she wanted that dam to break. If it did, would there ever be an end to it or would she flood the house? Instead of crying, she forced a smile and forged ahead, determined to power through.

Here's a fun fact about tears: They are cleansing. Refreshing. A visible demonstration of the pain leaking out. And that's a good thing because if you left it inside, you'd be like a volcano, always on the verge of erupting. (That sounds painful!)

Take a good look at today's quote from Henry Kissinger: "A diamond is a chunk of coal that did well under pressure." You're doing well under pressure. No, really. Give yourself some credit! After all you've been through, you deserve a meltdown from time to time. And who do you think created those tears, anyway? Remember, the Bible says that even Jesus wept.

So, let those tears flow. Get the feelings out. And remember, you can't move into a bright and beautiful tomorrow until you've dealt with the pain of the here and now. Today's cleansing tears will help you step into tomorrow's healthy possibilities.

AFFIRMATION

"My flesh and my heart may fail, but
God is the strength of my heart."
(Psalm 73:26 NIV)

ONE DUST BUNNY AT A TIME

If you have been harboring anger or bitterness or jealousy in your heart . . . hand it over to Christ, and ask Him to help you let it go.

Billy Graham

Cindy tidied up her office, ashamed of how messy she'd let it get. How did things pile up like that? Oh, right. When you worked as many hours as she did, it happened.

Exhausted, she finally took a seat at her desk to dive into a work-related spreadsheet. She happened to glance to her right and noticed, under a small table, dust bunnies on the floor, along with a couple of scraps of paper.

Really? How had she managed to overlook some of the mess, in spite of her seemingly thorough cleaning? A change of perspective had revealed the situation, and now she had no choice but to remedy it. The spreadsheet would have to wait.

Maybe you've been there. You've worked on certain areas of your life, tidying up. You've fixed the anger, the bitterness, the lack of self-control. Whew! You think you're all done with the hard work. Then something happens—a friend says something unkind, a child sasses you, your boss corrects you—and a Pandora's box is flung open. Unexpectedly harsh words, emotions, and attitudes soar out, zooming toward their intended target.

Whoa. Where did all that come from?

Girl, you've just discovered the hidden clutter under the table, and it must be dealt with. Those dust bunnies have to go!

Why do you suppose God forces us to look at those icky wisps of dust and torn scraps of paper? Because He's got bigger, better things ahead for us. He doesn't want us to get caught up in the debris of the past or the murky shadows of situations that no longer hold us in their grasp. Instead, He wants us freed up to soar, and that can only happen if we take the time to clean up the mess, one dust bunny at a time.

AFFIRMATION

I will let go of everything that is holding me back from soaring.

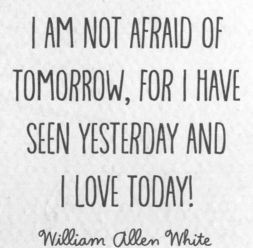

I AM NOT AFRAID OF
TOMORROW, FOR I HAVE
SEEN YESTERDAY AND
I LOVE TODAY!

William Allen White

GONE ON AHEAD

Now faith is confidence in what we hope for and
assurance about what we do not see.

Hebrews 11:1 NIV

Janetta opened the door to the curio cabinet
to dust the items inside. The moment she
saw the beautiful Scarlett O'Hara figurine, her
heart leaped to her throat. A gift from her father twenty-five years ago, the gorgeous piece
held a special place in her heart. Janetta's father
was long gone now, but the memories of how
he had surprised her that special day flooded
over her afresh. How thoughtful he had been.
How full of surprises.

For a moment she almost lost herself in the
bittersweet memories as sadness flooded over
her. Just as quickly, however, Janetta thought
about what her father would have said about
lingering in sadness and grief. "Janetta, there's
too much living to do. Don't look back. Only
look ahead."

As she thought about looking toward the future, a marvelous idea came to her. She would
take that gorgeous figurine and pass it on to her
grown daughter, in the hopes that it would one
day be passed to her granddaughter when she
was grown. Maybe they could keep the legacy
alive, along with the element of surprise. Yes,

perhaps she would deliver it with the very same note her father had written all those years ago.

Suddenly energized, Janetta rose and rushed to her jewelry box to find the note, which she'd kept safely tucked away. Tears flowed as she read her dad's words once more. She started to clean and wrap the beautiful figurine, then found a gift bag to put it in. Janetta could hardly wait to see the look of delight on her daughter's face when she opened it.

Perhaps, like Janetta, you've lost a parent or someone very special to you. All you have now are your memories and your keepsakes. Maybe it's time to keep the chain going. Is there a special something you can leave a child, a niece, or a nephew? Perhaps you could craft a loving note to be delivered with the item so that the legacy can go on and on. You'll bring such brightness to the ones you love as you pass that gift along.

AFFIRMATION

I can keep my family's legacy alive.

JUST BREATHE

You can't be brave if you've only had
wonderful things happen to you.

Mary Tyler Moore

Have you ever wondered why women are
taught Lamaze breathing techniques for
when they're in labor? When the pain is se-
vere, focusing on something else—anything,
really—helps. A lot.

In. Out. In. Out.

When you're fixated on the motion of the
breaths and your eyes are riveted to a random
spot on the wall, you're not thinking about
the pain.

In theory, anyway.

No doubt life has offered you plenty of la-
borious moments. Not the kind that produce a
child but the kind that eventually lead to something beautiful, if you can just press through
the pain without panicking or giving up. But
that's not always easy in the moment, is it?

Maybe you've heard the expression "Just
breathe!" If you're like most people, panic can
cause you to literally hold your breath. But
don't hold it for long. Even in the middle of a
crisis, *breathe:* In. Out. In. Out.

Breathing is the answer. When you face a crisis, allow the breath of the Holy Spirit to calm

you. He is your Comforter, you know. He's right there, ready to bind up your fears as you focus on Him.

Lynn learned this as she walked through a particularly tough experience with the IRS. A routine audit turned up unfounded accusations on their end, and she nearly panicked. (Talk about holding your breath!) Lynn got her breathing under control enough to pray about the situation and place it in God's hands. Before long, He pointed her in the direction of a good CPA, who helped her fight back—and win.

There will always be opportunities to panic. But remember, on the other side of the storms you usually find sunny skies and new possibilities. So, don't give up—and don't forget to breathe!

AFFIRMATION

Today I choose to believe that "perfect love casts out fear" (I John 4:18 ESV).

ROCKY ROAD FRIENDSHIPS

A little consideration, a little thought for
others, makes all the difference.

Eeyore

Ugh.
Robin hung up the phone, her stomach
in knots. Talking to her friend Pauline always
left her feeling this way. Up one minute, down
the next, they just couldn't seem to get off the
"reactions" roller coaster. And Pauline's volatile
temper didn't help. She overreacted to everything. At least, it felt that way to Robin.

Problem was, Pauline was an old friend.
Their relationship dated back to high school.
Yes, they were very different from each other
(boy, were they!), but Robin had always hoped
they could remain close. These days, she wasn't
so sure. The situation wasn't at the toxic point,
but things always seemed to escalate whenever
Pauline didn't get her way . . . which meant she
usually got her way. Robin often caved just to
keep the peace. Only that peace wasn't long-
lived. And she usually ended up feeling taken
advantage of or overlooked.

Maybe you've got a friend like that. (Maybe
you are a friend like that!) rocky road friendships are tough. Whether you're dealing with
personality conflicts or bigger issues, they're an

interruption to the norm and threaten to rob you of your peace. And those over-the-top reactions! Ouch!

There are some relationships that you really do need to walk away from. When you're dealing with manipulation, narcissism, or abuse of any kind, it's time to slam that door shut. Most relational issues, though, are just mild annoyances, not "See you never" situations.

Remember, you've probably provided equally as many "ugh" opportunities for your friends. Learning to adapt to different personalities can be tough! But those you love are worth it, so don't give up just yet unless the Lord has specifically nudged you to break off the relationship.

People aren't perfect. (Hint: you're a people too!) Relationships can be messy. But in those moments of bliss you'll be reminded that they are worth the effort.

AFFIRMATION

They're not perfect, but I choose to love them anyway.

THE MIRROR HAS TWO FACES

"The Lord doesn't see things the way you
see them. People judge by outward appearance,
but the Lord looks at the heart."

I Samuel 16:7 NLT

When you look in the mirror, who do you see? Not what, but who? Do you see the woman everyone else sees, or have you created a different persona in your mind, a woman that others could never love because of how she looks?

If so, you are definitely not alone. It's not unusual for gals of every shape, size, and color to beat themselves up over how they look, especially in the days of carefully angled, filtered photographs floating across social media. Most women see their beautiful friends and then hyper-focus on their own outward appearance, wishing they could change the bumps, wrinkles, and flaws.

If only they could, then others would find them acceptable. Lovable.

Take Lisa. After weeks of dieting, she'd only lost three pounds. With over thirty pounds left to lose, she still had a long way to go. It hardly seemed fair. Her husband could eat anything and never gain a pound, but if Lisa even looked at a candy bar, she put on weight.

Not that her husband seemed to notice or care that she was a little fluffier than when he'd married her. But she did. And whenever she was forced to look at her reflection in the mirror, Lisa grumbled and complained all over again.

Maybe you can relate. You're not a fan of how you look. For those who struggle with insecurities like weight or other physical attributes they wish they could change, coming to grips with their unfiltered reflection can be tough!

Oh, but God loves you just the way you are! He's not a beauty contest judge! He's not scoring you less because of your physical appearance. He couldn't care less about your freckles, wrinkles, or warts. Those things don't matter to Him.

He takes one look at you and says, "Well, hello there, gorgeous!" and He hopes you'll do the same!

AFFIRMATION

Today I refuse to let the mirror define me.

CORROSION

There are a hundred paths through the world that
are easier than loving. But, who wants easier?*

Mary Oliver

McKinsey decorated one of the walls in
her home's foyer with crosses in a variety
of sizes and styles. The large iron cross came as
a gift from a friend at church. The littlest one
was supposed to be a bookmark, but it looked
perfect with the others, hanging there in a field
of crosses. Perfection!

Every time she walked by the wall,
McKinsey stopped and gave them a closer look.
She remembered where every single one came
from. Some—like the big wrought iron one—
were heavier than others. The little silver one
was light in comparison.

Sometimes we feel like we have a lot of
crosses to bear. Our lives are like that wall—
filled with the heavy weights and the not-so-
heavy ones that seem to add up.

That elderly parent we have to take care of?
That's one cross. That moody husband who
never wants to do anything fun? That's another
cross. That kiddo who won't do anything you
tell him to do? That one seems huge. But the
great big one—the wrought iron cross that
troubles you daily . . . if you're like McKinsey,

you don't always talk about that one openly because the weight is just too much to bear.

McKinsey's marriage was in trouble, but no one knew. She and her husband did a terrific job of hiding their problems so that no one on the outside could tell. Their friends at church? Clueless. Her coworkers? They would be shocked to hear it. They heard McKinsey carry on about the kids, the latest vacation, the new home decor, and so on. They never heard about her husband's recent affair or his desire to leave for good.

Only when he chose to leave permanently was she forced to deal with that cross out in the open. (Nothing like having to come clean in a public way!) Doing so required opening up, talking to a counselor and a team of close friends who prayed her through. With their help, McKinsey was finally able to hand that cross off to the only One capable of carrying it—the One who died upon the cross to save her.

AFFIRMATION

I will give my crosses to the Savior, for He alone can carry them.

*Mary Oliver, New and Selected Poems, vol. 2 (Boston: Beacon Press, 2005), 173.

YOU ARE CORDIALLY INVITED . . .
TO A PITY PARTY!

Fear makes the wolf bigger than he is.

German proverb

Bridget knew how to throw a terrific pity party, complete with food and beverages. She would drown her sorrows in chips, donuts, and cocoa and then wonder why she felt miserable the next day.

Sometimes her parties would go on longer than expected. When loneliness set in, for example. When she felt overlooked by her husband, her kids, or her friends. When the boss demanded too much of her. When financial woes caused too big a sting. Anytime the wolf howled at her door, she responded by barring herself inside and going into pity-party mode. On those days, the party was wildly exaggerated. She ended up in worse shape at the end of the fiesta, once those bad food choices were made. (Ugh!)

Maybe you know what it's like to throw a pity party too. You pull out the streamers, reach for the sugary treats, and indulge while offering this common excuse: "I deserve it after all I've been through!"

Maybe it's time to ask God for a plan of action so that you don't knee-jerk next time. Remember, the wolf is rarely as big as he sounds when he's howling at the door. He's skilled in the art of intimidating potential victims, but that's about it. And also remember, he rarely gets through that door. So, many of the things you're fretting over won't actually come to pass. (Whew!) So instead of throwing ourselves into a frenzy and barring the doors, we can invite a friend over for coffee, take a walk, or spend a little quiet time with God.

A little pity partying is okay (in fact, sometimes it's downright needed), but it's always nice to think through other options that might leave you feeling a little better and maybe even a little stronger afterward.

AFFIRMATION

I will not hand the leash of my
life to a big, bad wolf.

TEMPER, TEMPER!

All of us fail, but this doesn't
mean that we are *failures.**

Robert McGee

Have you ever lost it? Like, really, really lost it? Maybe your toddler knocked over the bowl of spaghetti onto your freshly mopped floor and you hollered at him. Or, perhaps you had enough with your boss's pushiness and finally pushed back, but your words were laced with anger. It happens.

Some people seem to struggle more with anger than others. In fact, some make it a lifestyle . . . and they don't even seem to notice they're angry.

Such was the case with Brooke. Her husband, Charlie, was grumpy most of the time. People at church noticed. People at his job noticed. And the kids? Well, there was no hiding it from them. They weren't exactly scared of him but were very aware of his volatile temper. He could turn on a dime and ruin everyone's day.

Brooke wasn't sure how to handle it without making the situation worse. When things reached the point where she just couldn't go on wondering when the ever-bubbling volcano would finally erupt, Brooke reached out to someone on staff at her church. Charlie agreed to counseling, which surprised her.

- 38 -

Turned out, he wanted to see change in his life as much as she hoped to see it. The counseling got off to a rocky start. He countered her "You're always upset" argument by blaming her for triggering him. Only when the counselor—a trusted friend—said, "Charlie, you are pretty grumpy most of the time" did he see the truth. If others were noticing, no doubt he really was a grump.

Maybe you're grumpy too. Maybe you live on the edge of irritability all the time, the volcano threatening to erupt with lava pouring out on those you love, but don't know how to get past it. Often irritability is rooted in discontentment—sadness that your life hasn't turned out as you'd hoped. Perhaps it's time to acknowledge that before God and allow Him to bring the necessary healing.

And remember, there's nothing wrong with seeking out a counselor or close friend to share these burdens with. Only when you let go of the frustrations and discontentment of yesterday can you function better today and look forward to a brighter tomorrow.

AFFIRMATION

I will do my best to make the necessary changes to live life with hope and joy.

---

*Robert McGee, The Search for Significance: Seeing Your True Worth Through God's Eyes (Nashville: Thomas Nelson, 2003), 80.

A BRAVE NEW ENDING

Cure sometimes, treat often, comfort always.

Hippocrates

Annie sat in the chair next to her best friend as Kay received the dreadful news: Pancreatic cancer. Stage four.

Kay's eyes were riveted to the doctor, who sat across from them with a somber look on his face.

"I've suspected for some time, which is why I've been running so many tests over the past couple of weeks," Dr. Jamison explained, his words compassionate and kind. "I'm sorry to say my suspicions turned out to be right."

The next few minutes—and hours—were a blur. Annie let Kay lead the way in the conversation that followed the doctor's visit. And, as they drove home, Annie tried to think of the right things to say, but nothing helpful came to her. How could she comfort her best friend after news like that?

Turned out, Kay did lead the way, in more ways than Annie had imagined. In spite of not feeling well, Kay spent the next few weeks enjoying life to the full. She took her granddaughter on a kayak ride at a nearby lake. She celebrated her birthday at a pizza joint with a large group of boisterous friends. She settled her financial matters so the family wouldn't be burdened. And even as the situation grew more painful, she kept everyone entertained with her antics while hospitalized. Every single day she kept Jesus front and center.

Kay ended her journey on Planet Earth with these words on her lips: "I can't wait to see Jesus." And she meant it. She died, just as she had lived, with a passion for her Savior and a heart filled with love.

Through Kay's courage, her friends—including Annie—learned how to face each day just as she had.

Maybe you've had a friend like Kay. Her bravery astounded you. We have so much to learn from those who teach us how to have brave new endings. Oh, how wonderful to live among friends who love Jesus and point us to Him, even in the hardest of situations!

AFFIRMATION

No matter what I face,
I can live with courage and joy,
blessing those I love.

THERE ARE FAR,
FAR BETTER THINGS
AHEAD THAN ANY WE
LEAVE BEHIND.

C.S. Lewis

UGH!

We must accept finite disappointment,
but never lose infinite hope.

Martin Luther King Jr.

Corinne had a plan for how everything would work out. She would pick up her daughter from the airport at 7:45, swing back home to pick up her husband and the other kids, and then, together, they would all head out to her daughter's favorite restaurant for a late birthday dinner. If she had planned everything right, they would have just enough time for a quick meal before the restaurant closed.

Only, evening traffic made her late to the airport. And when she got there, Corinne learned her daughter's flight had been delayed. Ugh! Half an hour later, she was still waiting.

Her beautiful daughter emerged exactly forty-seven minutes later than expected, all smiles. She had no idea about the planning that had gone into making her birthday special. She was just glad to be home from college to spend time with the family on her big day.

A short while later the whole family sat in a fast-food joint that happened to be open late. Corinne felt like crying because things had gone so far south, but that sweet, oblivious daughter of hers didn't seem to notice or care.

She and her siblings were having one laugh after another as she shared funny antics of things that had happened back at school.

Corinne finally relaxed when she realized that God had taken the situation and turned it around in His own special way.

Don't you love that difference in perspective? When we face those "Ugh!" moments, we can get wound up or we can relax and enjoy the ride. The very moments we find frustrating often turn out to be memory makers. So, don't fret when things don't work out the way you planned. Likely, God's got something bigger and better in mind!

AFFIRMATION

My hope is in the Lord,
not my circumstances.

SAFE ZONE

The cave you fear to enter holds
the treasure you seek.

Joseph Campbell

Sharen couldn't stop trembling as she followed closely behind her husband into the damp, dark cave. Why she'd let him talk her into this, she could not say. For years he'd wanted to visit the underground caverns in Central Texas, but the idea of going down, down, down under the ground into a shadowy, tightly enclosed space did not sound appealing . . . at all.

She reluctantly gave in when their vacation travels led them directly past the caverns. And now, here she was—husband in front of her, three kiddos behind her, hand tightly clutched in case she slipped or fell.

When they reached their first stopping point, the tour guide pointed out the mineral deposits called stalactites hanging from the ceiling above. She stared in awe at the beautiful teardrops, jagged and intricately carved by the finger of God. Wow. Then the guide pointed out the stalagmites, growing up from the bottom of the cave—upside-down teardrops of mineral deposits, twinkling with drops of water.

How had she missed this all her life? Oh, right. She had allowed fear to keep her from entering "the scary place." Only, now that she was actually here, it wasn't scary at all.

Maybe you're afraid of the scary places too. That financial matter you don't want to look at. That church choir solo you're afraid to audition for. That airplane you're afraid to get on. Those caverns you're frightened to visit.

Life offers a zillion opportunities to say, "No thank you. I'd rather not! I prefer to stay in my safe zone, thank you very much!"

But sometimes, if you take the hand of someone nearby and surround yourself with loved ones who boost your courage, you really can enter the scary places. And once there? Well, you might just be surrounded by breathtaking moments of unexpected beauty.

AFFIRMATION

I will explore the scary places.

PALPABLE

The adventure of the Christian life
begins when we dare to do what we
would never tackle without Christ.

William Penn

W hat would Steven want you to do?"
Gillian looked up as her friend Paula
asked the question. "What do you mean?"

"I mean . . ." Paula gave her a pensive look.
"Steven was adventurous. Fun. And together,
you were a force to be reckoned with, always
off on some adventure or another. Now that
he's gone . . ."

Her words drifted off and Gillian sighed.
"Now that he's gone I'm not the same? Is that
what you mean?"

"It's to be expected. You're grieving." Paula
reached over and gave Gillian's hand a squeeze.
"But I think Steven would want you to go on
with those little adventures you used to have.
Those road trips. The cruises. The big family
theme parties. All of that."

"By myself?"

"No." Paula grinned. "With me. I'll be adventurous with you. I think it sounds like fun.
Well, as long as you don't make me jump out of
a plane or bungee jump or anything like that."

Gillian laughed at the image that presented.

"That's the first time I've heard you laugh in ages." Paula's lips tipped up in a smile. "So, what do you say? Are you in? Want to be adventure buddies? Because I, for one, think it sounds like a blast!"

Gillian thought about it for a second before nodding. "I'm in," she said at last. "You're right, Paula. Steven would want me to go on living."

"Not just living, but truly living every single moment to the fullest." Paula offered an encouraging nod. "That's how he was, and that's how you're meant to be."

Maybe you find yourself in Gillian's story. You've lost your spouse and you wonder if all the adventure has gone out of your story. You think your best days are behind you.

Half the journey is in deciding your best days are not behind you. Your loved one wouldn't want you stuck in a rut. So, begin to look at tomorrow as a bright, adventurous place, filled with possibilities and wonder.

AFFIRMATION

I am whole, not half.

EMPTY SUITCASES

God doesn't need a lot to do a lot. All David had
was five stones. And all David used was one.

Tony Evans

When Mary was a little girl, she dreamed of owning a record player. One Christmas when she was five years old, she opened a beautifully wrapped present that appeared to be her dream gift. Sure enough! The case was just the right size. It had to be!

Only, when she opened it, she discovered the case was empty inside.

A suitcase. Her parents had given her a little wooden suitcase. Didn't they realize the gift she really wanted? Hadn't she dropped enough clues?

Mary was devastated, of course. But, over time, that little suitcase became one of her favorite toys. She filled it with doll clothes. She used it to pack up her personal items when spending the night at her grandmother's house. She lugged all sorts of things around in it. And when she went off to college, she had to fight the temptation to take that little case with her. Instead, she packed it away in her parents' attic so that it would remain safe until she could pass it on to her daughter someday.

That's how life is sometimes. We get our

hopes up, and then they're dashed. We're as devastated as that five-year-old with the empty suitcase. Didn't we plant enough clues for God to figure out what we really wanted? Why would He let us down and give us something other than what we thought was best?

Here's a precious truth (learned only by experience): If we'll allow Him to, God will begin to show us the wonder of what's inside those so-called empty cases He places into our hands—all the things we didn't notice at first glance. And, if we're really paying attention, we'll begin to see that what He's offering is far more valuable than anything we might have asked for.

He'll take the empty containers of our hearts and fill them in wondrous ways, if we let Him.

AFFIRMATION

When I feel empty, He's right there, waiting to fill me.

LET'S RUMBLE

I understand now that the vulnerability I've always
felt is the greatest strength a person can have. You
can't experience life without feeling life. What I've
learned is that being vulnerable to someone you
love is not a weakness. It's a strength.

Elisabeth Shue

I don't want to talk about it."

Ginger pushed the food around on her
plate with her fork. Why did Aggie always
feel the need to pry into things that weren't
her business?

"Ginger, I just think it would help if you
opened up and talked about it, that's all." Aggie
rested her hand on Ginger's, and for the first
time Ginger realized that her friend probably
wasn't prying after all. She just wanted to help.
Like the last time . . . and the time before.

"You always push me away." Aggie's eyes
misted over. "And I get it. The stuff you're going through is hard to talk about. But please
know that I'm right here when you're ready."

Ginger set the fork down and released a slow
breath. Was this the day she finally came clean
and told someone about the depression she'd
been walking through? Would Aggie—whose
life seemed perfect in comparison—understand? Or would she judge her?

Based on the compassion in her friend's eyes right now, she would understand.

"You ready to rumble?" Aggie asked.

"Rumble?"

"Mm-hmm. Get it all out. Because I'm here, if you are. And I've got all the time in the world."

After a moment's pause, Ginger began the difficult task of opening up. Finally. She made herself vulnerable to her best friend. Okay, so she also soaked a napkin with her tears, but the waiter didn't seem to mind. Neither did Aggie, who only listened and responded in love and offered to pray with her—right there in the restaurant.

Wow. Why had she waited so long to open up?

Maybe you're like Ginger. You don't like to expose yourself to others for fear they won't get it. But there's a reason the Bible says to lay down your worries, fears, regrets, pains, and sorrows. Being vulnerable can lead to a happier future. And remember, you can always turn to Jesus. He's the best load-carrier there is!

AFFIRMATION

I will try to look at vulnerability as a good thing.

MY BRAIN IS BROKEN

For I am a bear of very little brain,
and long words bother me.

Winnie the Pooh

Ever had a day so off-kilter that you felt like your brain was broken? Maybe you had so many items on your to-do list that the whole thing felt overwhelming, so you couldn't figure out where to start.

Margaret had that problem. Her tiny town-home was overrun with clutter. Each day the problem grew worse. She had no organizational system, so stuff went, well, everywhere.

One day, she finally decided she'd had enough. Today she would dive in.

Only, she couldn't figure out where to start. If she moved the items from the hall closet to the garage, then she would have to tackle the mess in the garage to fit them in. And if she tackled the mess in the garage, then she would be forced to examine those boxes with all her deceased grandmother's personal items.

The more she thought about it, the muddier it all became in her mind. Maybe she should just wait until another day.

No matter how big the mess you've created in your personal space, there's a way out. Even if you're a clutter-bug and things are in a chaotic state, there are still brighter days ahead for you.

Start with a list of all the things that need to be done, then spend some time praying over that list. God will show you which items to tackle first. Then remember that old adage: "How do you eat an elephant? One bite at a time!" Tackle one or two items on your list every day. Or work on one room per day. Or one closet per day. The Lord will download a plan that makes sense to your schedule.

For sure, He has a better way than living in chaos. That's no fun! Your bright future includes a safe, healthy living environment, one that doesn't cause you distress. Before long you'll be cozied up on the sofa with a cup of tea in hand, looking around at your beautiful, organized space.

AFFIRMATION

When my heart is overwhelmed
and my brain is feeling broken,
I will lean on the Great Organizer!

THE VALLEY SO LOW

I have been asked hundreds of times in my life why God allows tragedy and suffering. I have to confess that I really do not know the answer totally, even to my own satisfaction. I have to accept, by faith, that God is sovereign, and He is a God of love and mercy and compassion in the midst of suffering.

Billy Graham

Depression is more than a "low" feeling. It's more than a day or two of exhaustion on the sofa binge-watching your favorite TV series. True clinical depression can interrupt your life in a major way, affecting relationships, your job, and even your ability to pay bills.

Robin wasn't sure what to call the season she was walking through. She had no "significant event" to blame it on. No relational breakup. No job loss or home foreclosure. Nothing big. But she just couldn't seem to pull herself up from the pit.

Her emotions were more volatile than usual, tears came more easily, and her energy level hit rock bottom. When a friend invited her out to lunch—something she would normally love to do—Robin just couldn't make herself go. She didn't have the energy. Instead, she nibbled on cookies and watched another pointless episode of a show she didn't even really like.

Maybe you've been there and you weren't

sure how to lift yourself out of the doldrums. People said things like, "You have so much to be happy about" or "Your life is great! Why moan and groan?" but you couldn't seem to stop.

Check out this encouraging verse from Jeremiah 29:11 (ESV): "For I know the plans I have for you, declares the LORD, plans for welfare and not for evil, to give you a future and a hope." When you recognize that He's got big plans for all your tomorrows, it makes you want to do more than just trudge through today.

And remember, there's nothing shameful in admitting you need help. Reach out to a counselor, and if needed, visit a doctor for a workup.

God has big, bright things in store for you, and it's time to walk back out into the sunlight again.

AFFIRMATION

I will fight the temptation to dwell in the valley.

TRUE SELVES

What we know matters, but
who we are matters more.

Brené Brown

"W ho are you?" If someone asked you
that question, would you know how
to answer?

You might say, "My name is so-and-so."

Or maybe, "I'm Bobby and Cindy's mom."

You might respond with, "I'm a teacher" or
"I work at a doctor's office."

If you're married, you might say, "I'm married
to Joe."

But none of those things define you. Until
you know who you really are—not what you
do or whom you're related to—you will struggle
to know your place in the world.

Before there was a husband or kids or a job,
even before you drew your first breath, you
were a child of the Most High God. And you're
still His kid, even now. Once you realize Whose
you are, you can know who you are.

When you come to fully understand
what that means, when you have rooted and
grounded your identity in Him, then your
response to the "Who are you?" question will
be made easier.

Knowing who you are will help you stick to your guns when you need to. But most of all, you'll have the assurance that the same God who created daffodils, cumulus clouds, crystal-blue Caribbean seas, and teensy-tiny tadpoles created you. And He adores you with a love that goes beyond anything you could imagine.

This loving, gracious Creator has big things planned for you. The reason you can be assured of the fact that you have brighter days ahead is because He's the one illuminating them. And no one does a finer job of lighting your path than He does!

AFFIRMATION

Today I choose to recognize Whose I am so that I can fully understand who I am.

THOSE WHO HOPE IN THE
LORD WILL RENEW THEIR
STRENGTH. THEY WILL SOAR
ON WINGS LIKE EAGLES;
THEY WILL RUN AND NOT
GROW WEARY, THEY WILL
WALK AND NOT BE FAINT.

Isaiah 40:31 NIV

SHADOWS

It never hurts to keep looking for sunshine.

Eeyore

Scarlet curled up in her bed in the dark bedroom, listening to the wind howl outside. She could hear the sound of the sleet hitting the windows but could see nothing. The power had gone out thirty minutes ago. She prayed it would come back on soon, but with ice and snow covering the ground and the temperatures in the low teens, Scarlet wondered how—or if—she would see power anytime soon. It was well past midnight now. Others in the neighborhood were likely fast asleep, unaware of the darkness. But she couldn't rest her heart or mind.

How long could she keep her house warm in these conditions? And what about all the food in the refrigerator and freezer? She'd cooked soup in preparation for the cold snap. Would it all be wasted if the power didn't come back on? And how would she keep her two dogs warm?

After fretting for several minutes, Scarlet finally relaxed. God hadn't fallen off His throne. She had plenty of warm clothes and blankets. Her pups had sweaters. They could cuddle together in bed until the storm passed. And even if it lingered more than a few hours, her phone was charged. Her gas stove could still heat up soup once she used the lighter to get it going. Everything would end well, no matter how many hours—or even days—it took. She could trust God, even in the middle of the storm.

Maybe you've been in a storm like that. You felt isolated. Alone. Discombobulated. But then you remembered, "Hey, God hasn't fallen off His throne. He's still right there, doing what He always does—holding things together." Those endless nights, the ones that seem to go on forever? They really don't. The sun always breaks through in radiant splendor, and life goes on in glorious display. So hold on through the storm. The morning is coming.

AFFIRMATION

I serve a God who can see in the dark.

WHEN PRAYING SEEMS POINTLESS

When God says no, we are sometimes tempted
to wonder if He loves us. In reality, it's because He
loves us, He sometimes says no.

Lysa TerKeurst

Have you ever been in a situation where prayer seemed pointless, where crying out to God felt like a futile endeavor? Maybe you've been through a crisis in the past and felt let down by His response . . . or what appeared to be His lack of response. Or, maybe He answered no to a prayer and you got discouraged, so you decided to skip out on praying the next time.

Oh, sweet child of God! Prayer is a lifeline to your Creator, your one true link to the supernatural intervention of the only One who can help. Cutting Him out is the equivalent of cutting off your oxygen supply or shutting down the power to your house.

Don't cut that link, no matter how pointless praying might seem in the moment. If you could only see the things God is up to behind that invisible veil, you would be so excited! He's already putting plans in order, players in place, and hearts in motion. There's a heavenly chess game going on that you aren't able to see, but here's a fun fact: you're going to win this game.

You will. Even if things don't work out exactly as you might hope, you're going to come out stronger, healthier, more capable. And guess what else happens when you pray? It bolsters your confidence in the God of heaven and earth. Each day, as you stand in faith, you are growing into His own image. When that happens, you can believe for the impossible.

What seems impossible today? Have you stopped praying about it? Did you give up? Perhaps it's time to pick back up again so that your precious heavenly Father can prove once again that your prayers—no matter how repetitive—are never pointless.

AFFIRMATION

I choose to believe that God hears my prayers and will answer in His time.

THE SMALLEST OF MOMENTS

Keep your eyes on the stars and
your feet on the ground.

Theodore Roosevelt

Cora was stuck at home, dealing with COVID symptoms. Living alone was tough enough during a regular, healthy season, but when facing something of this magnitude? She felt the aloneness more than ever. The first couple of days she wondered what it would be like to have someone close to take care of her. Would she ever know that feeling?

After several rough days, she finally felt well enough to tend to some things around the house. While filling the dishwasher she realized she'd neglected taking the trash to the curb . . . for over a week! And the can was loaded.

She waited until late at night, when everyone nearby would be sound asleep . . . just in case she was still contagious. Then she ventured outside to wheel the can to the curb. Clack, clack, clack . . . down the driveway she went with the noisy can, probably waking everyone in the neighborhood. Ugh.

As she came back up the driveway, Cora happened to glance up . . . and gasped. The night sky was brilliant, twinkling lights filling it in a wondrous display of God's handiwork. What she hadn't noticed with her hands full of trash, she now saw clearly.

Cora paused and stared up, overcome by the beauty of it all. Off in the distance a lovely moon hung low, a perfect orb of radiant light. It guided her back up the driveway and into the house once more.

Isn't that just how life is sometimes? You're down, feeling alone, doing the most mundane thing. And then God shows up and shows off in the most marvelous way! You don't notice it at first because you're dealing with the icky stuff. But when you release those things into His hands, He proves to you that He was right there all along, even when you felt alone.

AFFIRMATION

Today I will look for sparkling moments.

A PLACE TO BELONG

Friendship is born at that moment
when one person says to another, "you too?
I thought I was the only one."

C.S. Lewis

Anita loved her little foster dog, Gabriel. He was the cutest little thing—a terrier mix with black and white fur and deep brown eyes. The little darling had been rescued off the streets. He was skinny and frail and completely unsocialized. No one knew how long he'd been wandering around out there, but Anita was so happy to have him with her now. He arrived at her home on December 18, just before Christmas, so she gave him the name Gabriel. He earned it with his stellar behavior.

Not long after Gabe's arrival, Anita got sick with the flu. She couldn't leave her house for several days, and the little dog provided just the right amount of company. He loved to snuggle and cuddle, just what she needed. And he didn't require much care—just some food, water, and a few tummy tickles kept him satisfied.

At the end of her illness, Anita knew she couldn't let this little guy go. She would have to adopt him and make him her furr-ever pup.

Maybe you feel a bit like Gabriel. You haven't really fit in anywhere, though not for lack of trying. You're like a pup wandering the streets, feeling like you don't have a place to belong. Those women at work, the ones who are always going out to lunch together? Why don't they invite you? Your two sisters? They seem close to each other but not to you. That neighbor you've tried to connect with? Why is she always so busy?

Oh, but don't give up just yet! Like Gabriel, the perfect fit is ahead. That sweet pup wasn't meant to walk alone, and neither are you. There will be friends, companions, confidants . . . all you could want and more. But you have to keep putting yourself out there to meet the perfect ones. When you do, it will be as cozy and comfortable as Gabriel and Anita, curled up on the sofa together.

AFFIRMATION

Great relationships are worth waiting for.

THE SUPERHIGHWAY

When everything you've hoped and prayed for
doesn't happen the way you thought it would, rest
your weary heart and know that God is drawing
you close to Him and He is not abandoning your
dreams. He is holding your heart close to His.

Katy Fults

Bridget loved the elephant ear plants that her husband put in the back garden. They were luscious and green and filled the space with beauty. When it rained, droplets formed on those big, vibrant leaves and glistened in the afternoon sunlight. More than anything, they reminded her of a trip she'd once taken to a tropical paradise.

Every winter they would die off and her husband would trim them back. But then in the spring there they were again, in all their glory . . . bigger and more vibrant than ever. Those gorgeous plants took her breath away. They also energized her and made her want to work harder on the rest of her garden.

Maybe you've had dreams like that. They started off big and beautiful. Then an unexpected winter season came along and drove them into the ground. They died off and you thought you would never see a resurrection season. After a while, you gave up.

Let's face it: Dreams don't always come true. People don't always catch the vision for the things you hope to accomplish. But that doesn't mean you should give up. Even during seasons when those elephant ears die off, there's the anticipation that they will return in the spring. When the warmth of the sun breaks through . . . bam! Spring! Suddenly the possibilities stretch out in front of you like a superhighway stretching into the great beyond.

God has plenty of springtimes ahead for you. This is just a wintry spell. That ice will melt, and when it does . . . look out! The superhighway will call your name!

AFFIRMATION

I won't give up on my dreams,
even during the winter seasons.

LET DOWN THE LOAD

Don't underestimate the value of Doing Nothing,
of just going along, listening to all the things you
can't hear, and not bothering.

A. A. Milne

Fran dreamed of hiking in the Rocky Mountains. She talked her husband into a trip to nearby Estes Park, a lovely, scenic village. Their plan? To hike during the day and enjoy the town in the evenings and mornings.

Their first day on the hiking trail, Fran found herself regretting her decision—not to hike but to carry the backpack filled with so much stuff. They weren't really going that deep into the mountains, so why did she need so many provisions? Maybe she'd over-prepared, if such a thing was possible.

A careful reassessment took place once they returned to the hotel that evening. The next day she went with a smaller, lighter pack. It held only the things she might actually use, should an emergency arise. They kept to well-marked trails and didn't venture far out, just in case.

Fortunately, they didn't need any of their provisions except food and water and a bandage for a blister on her foot. She happened to have one in her pack.

Can you relate to Fran's trailblazer plight? Have you ever carried a heavy load? Uphill? In rough terrain? Maybe it's time to ask God to remove everything that is weighing you down. Cast off the weight that so easily besets you, hems you in, causing you to freeze in place. Hand that pack to Jesus and watch Him carry the load for you. Before long you'll be breezing up the trail, leaving your worries in the dust.

AFFIRMATION

Today I choose to step away
from the chaos and just be.

POCKETBOOK WOES

My flesh and my heart may fail, but God is the
strength of my heart and my portion forever.

Psalm 73:26 NIV

Whenever Lila would get stressed out over
her finances, she would bake. Cookies. Cakes. Brownies. Pies. Didn't matter.
Stress called for baking. There was something
about being in the kitchen, creating something tasty and beautiful, that made everything
better again.

Unwilling to eat all her baked goods, she
started taking them to work to share with
coworkers. Before long, they started asking
for more.

"That chocolate cake you brought last
Tuesday was the best I've ever eaten. Would
you bake one for my husband's birthday next
month? I'll pay you."

"Girl, I've never had cupcakes decorated
as pretty as the ones you brought in for
Valentine's Day. Could I get you to make
some for my daughter's graduation? I'd rather
give you the money than the grocery store or
local bakery."

"Those oatmeal cookies were better than
my grandmother's, but don't tell her I said so,
okay? Could you bake a couple dozen for my
book club?"

It didn't take long to see that God was providing a way past some of the financial woes, and He used her existing gift to do it. With the additional income from baking, she was able to get caught up on that credit card debt. And, once caught up, she kept right on baking and tucking money aside for a rainy day. She also had a blast learning more about the craft and furthering her skills.

Lila would say that God turned lemons into lemonade. Or, in this case . . . lemon-blueberry cake. With a yummy glaze on top.

What has you stressed out today? Finances? Car troubles? Work problems? Remember, like Lila, the Lord already sees the solution, long before you do. Ask Him to download His plan, so that you can rest easy in His provision, even before you see it with your own eyes. And don't be surprised if He uses a gift He's already been stirring up.

AFFIRMATION

I won't allow my bank balance
to rob me of my joy.

NO PERMANENT BLOTS

We need to understand that failing
can be a step toward maturity, not a
permanent blot on our self-esteem.*

Robert McGee

Jane let out a cry as she saw the black marks
all over her brand-new French Provincial
bedroom suite. She turned to discover her
three-year-old daughter with a marker in hand.
Her clothing and face were also covered.

"Oh, Trisha! How could you?" Jane pulled
the marker from her hand and rushed her to
the bathroom to scrub the stains off.

Only, they wouldn't come off, no matter
how hard she scrubbed. Neither would they
come off her once-gorgeous white furniture.
She did her best, but there was no removing
those black marks.

It took days for Trisha to look normal, but
years went by and the furniture never did. It
stood as a testament to her daughter's naughti-
ness (and Mom's punishment for getting too
wrapped up in a phone call to notice).

Maybe you've experienced something like
that. Maybe a beautiful dress was ruined because of one spill. Maybe a dress shirt got an
ink stain in the pocket. Maybe the couch had a
spot where the dog chewed through the fabric.

Hey, these things happen! But they really can wreck your day (or even your week or year, depending on the cost of the destruction).

Those permanent blots are reminders of the bad thing that happened. Every time you see them, you relive the event all over again. Ugh! Sometimes the only way to get rid of the memories is to toss the item or (in the case of the furniture) to paint over the stains in the hopes that you can hide them.

Aren't you glad there are no permanent blots on your record? As soon as you asked Jesus to remove them, He did! He doesn't look at you and see black marks. No, when he looks at you, He sees French Provincial all the way.

Because God forgives and forgets, you can move forward with confidence and joy. There's nothing to hold you back. Your record is clean!

AFFIRMATION

It's never too late to begin again.

*Robert McGee, The Search for Significance: Seeing Your True Worth Through God's Eyes (Nashville: Thomas Nelson, 2003), 80.

COURAGE IS CONTAGIOUS.
WHEN A BRAVE MAN
TAKES A STAND, THE
SPINES OF OTHERS ARE
OFTEN STIFFENED.

Billy Graham

BULLETS

We are here to thrive. Not to sometimes survive.

Ezinne Orjiako, Nkem

There's always that one person. You know the one. She takes advantage of you at work. And then, after bad-mouthing and mistreating you, she takes the credit for all you've done.

It makes your stomach curdle, the way she brags about how she manages the best department on the team. You want to rat her out to the boss, but he's so busy he wouldn't really pay much attention. And what would he do about it, anyway? He just wants to get the job done and move on. Thanks to your hard work, the job is getting done, so he's a happy man. But you? You're exhausted.

You decide to keep quiet, but inside you're seething. You work harder than anyone else, but that doesn't stop this woman from harassing you, carrying on about how you could do better. Her words are like bullets to the heart. And for what? So that her star can shine brighter? Hardly seems fair.

It's hard to know how to thrive in situations like this, but remember . . . you are where you are for a reason. And if it's the wrong reason—

if you're really meant to be someplace else—God will show you. He will give you a way out.

In the meantime, know that you've got a bright future and she can't rob you of that, so don't waste your thoughts on her antics. Just do the best job you can under the circumstances and grow in faith and experience. And if the right opportunity presents itself (pray about it!), you might find an open door to talk to your boss privately. Instead of walking in with a heart full of bullet holes, you'll be able to face him with strength and dignity.

AFFIRMATION

Today I refuse to allow those bullets to permeate my heart.

CRACKS IN THE EARTH

To the brave and brokenhearted who
have taught us how to rise after we fall.
Your courage is contagious.*

Brené Brown

Susan couldn't make any sense out of the things her sister was saying. The words were nonsensical, filled with bizarre details. And her sister's over-the-top animation troubled her almost as much. This wasn't the first time she'd heard Karen talk like this or get so wound up about things that made no sense to anyone else. From time to time her younger sister would get extremely agitated and go off on a tangent in dramatic fashion. And it never made sense, any of it.

Sometimes things ended with Karen getting angry and threatening. Those incidents were frightening. Susan suspected mental illness but didn't know how to broach the subject. After one particularly frightening episode where her sister began throwing valuables away, Susan decided to approach Karen's husband to get his take on things.

Turned out, he was relieved someone else had noticed. Together they managed to talk Karen into going to a psychiatrist, where she was diagnosed with schizophrenia. After getting on the medication things calmed down, but after a while they started up again. The next few years were like a pendulum, swinging back and forth. When Karen stayed on her meds, things weren't bad, but then she would think she was cured and would stop the medication altogether. Things would go off the rails again.

Maybe you're loving a family member or friend through a similar crisis. It's hard to know what to do when someone you love is struggling with mental illness. God never meant for us to walk this road alone.

That's why you've got to have help. You need a team of trusted people who know what they're doing. This is one road you were never meant to walk alone.

AFFIRMATION

The cracks are deep, but
God's love is deeper still.

*Brené Brown, Rising Strong: How the Ability to Reset Transforms the Way We Live, Love, Parent, and Lead (New York: Random House, 2015).

GOOD CHRISTIANS

No relationship is all sunshine, but two can share
one umbrella and weather the storm together.

Anonymous

Have you ever felt like you didn't fit in with the church crowd? Sometimes those folks can be a little too, well . . . perfect. Or so they seem. You don't hear them saying the wrong thing or doing the wrong thing. Their kids aren't in trouble at school or facing down a police officer for damaging someone else's property. No, their kiddos are on the honor roll or volunteering in the nursery at church. Their husbands? Leading the men's Bible study, of course.

Want a Scripture, verse? This practically-perfect-in-every-way gal has one on the tip of her tongue at all times, always appropriate to the situation. Need a ride to the doctor or a hot meal when you're sick? She's got you covered. Need someone to step up and take charge of the women's Christmas banquet at church? She's your gal, and she comes complete with Pinterest-worthy decorating skills. (Did she miss her calling as an interior decorator, perhaps?)

Where did you go wrong? How come you didn't get the perfect Christian life like she did?

You've done your best, after all. But you can barely find time to cook a meal for yourself, let alone deliver one to a sick family. And when you quote a Bible verse it's usually something like, "Vengeance is mine; I will repay, saith the Lord" (Romans 12:19 KJV). You've got that one memorized. You want to volunteer at church, but who has time for all that? You're not getting enough sleep as it is.

Maybe she is practically perfect in every way. But you know what? External appearances (especially a churchy facade) can be deceiving. More likely she's far from the picture of perfection you've painted in your head.

But even if she really is as amazing as she seems, so are you! God is using you to bring a smile to others and to lift their spirits with your crazy antics. Not everyone is made to fit in. So, don't work so hard to be like everyone else. Let them get to know you just as you are—flawed, imperfect, wonderful you.

AFFIRMATION

I wasn't meant to fit in. God designed me to stand out.

NO SUGARCOATING

Instead, we will speak the truth in love,
growing in every way more and more like Christ,
who is the head of his body, the church.

Ephesians 4:15 NLT

Mirabelle paced the room and tried to think of a way to share the story with her husband. He needed to know that their son had been expelled from school for getting into a fight with another boy. But Robert wouldn't take it well. They'd been through this sort of thing before. Multiple times, in fact.

Still, there was no sugarcoating the story. She couldn't very well un-suspend her son, now could she? Robert would have to know, and she had to be the one to tell him.

Maybe you've been in a rough situation like that, where you had to share not-so-great news with someone you loved. You couldn't think of a way to transition with ease into the subject, so you just blurted it out.

Usually getting the truth out there is better than beating around the bush, anyway. Whether it's telling your husband about that big purchase you put on the credit card or admitting to your boss that you made a huge accounting error during the last billing cycle— getting things over with is always best.

And while you're at it, it's time to have that "hard talk" with your son, as well. You know the one. Instead of dancing around his issues, you've got to speak the truth in love so that he grows up into a healthy, stable man, not one who pushes others around.

Is it easy to speak hard truths? No. (And you might be quivering as you think about how hard it might be.) But it's always worth it. Friendships can be saved. Marriages can be healed. Work relationships can be restored. Children's lives can be changed. Addicted friends can be set free.

All of this and more . . . when you speak the truth in love.

AFFIRMATION

It's not going to be easy,
but I will do my best to speak the truth
in love, then watch for a miracle!

TURN, TURN, TURN

Circumstances are the rulers of the weak;
they are but the instruments of the wise.

Samuel Lover

If you've learned anything from the COVID-19 season, it's this: nothing is predictable. Everything is subject to change, often without notice. You can make all the plans you like, but—in the blink of an eye—everything can shift. Precious opportunities might slip through your fingers.

That trip you had planned? Looks like it's off. That family holiday you had hoped to host? Not happening. Your daughter's much-anticipated graduation from high school? Ugh. That one really hurt.

So, how do you handle it when the unexpected things happen? When you're faced with a sudden financial woe or an unwanted health crisis? How do you manage when your plans for a vacation are thwarted or a job opportunity slips through your fingers? Change isn't easy. It takes a lot of energy to stop something you're doing, completely rethink your plan, and go a different way. But you can do it! You're learning from these disappointments. A lot.

Did you learn some lessons from 2020, perhaps? Part of what makes life so adventurous is not knowing how things will turn out. But if you're a control freak, not knowing what is around the corner can be scary. Maybe it's time to learn how to "let go and let God." The year 2020 might have looked like letdown after letdown, but even those who've been the most disappointed still have a bright future.

Things happen. Life happens. Unavoidable circumstances happen. But you can't allow those things to control how you feel about your future. It's just as bright as it ever was (copper penny bright, in fact). So, don't give in to those feelings of hopelessness. They are, after all, just feelings.

Will you allow God to take the mess and turn it into a hopeful message for the days ahead?

AFFIRMATION

Today I refuse to stress myself out about things I cannot control or change.

THIS IS A TEST

The truth of the matter is, this too will pass,
and we'll get through it with more peace and
stability if we'll trust God to do what is best for
us at the right time and in His way.

Joyce Meyer

Pop quizzes weren't Linda's thing. Once,
in Bible college, she found herself facing
a pop quiz in her Old Testament survey class.
She hadn't read the text and was completely
clueless as to the answers.

Who were King David's sons? She had
no idea.

In a moment of what she thought was
sheer brilliance, she penciled in "Larry, Moe,
and Curly."

Unfortunately, her professor didn't find her
answers as funny as she did. She got a very low
score on the pop quiz, which brought her over-
all grade down.

As much as we try to avoid them, life is filled
with pop quizzes. Boy, can they ever come
along at just the wrong time. Whether you
pass or fail them, there's always something to
be learned.

There are relational tests, faith tests, even financial tests. And though you often come out
of them feeling like a failure, there's no "pass
or fail" with God. He's simply hoping you

learn and grow from the testing seasons you walk through.

Courtney did. She and her husband went through a rough patch when they lost their home to foreclosure. Really, the situation couldn't be avoided. Zach became ill and lost his job. They fell behind on the mortgage and—even after he recovered from his illness—couldn't get caught back up.

In the throes of it, Courtney did her best not to panic. She sent letters and emails to the mortgage company, offering to work things out, but they did not respond as she'd hoped.

God opened a door for a rental home that was considerably larger than the house they were losing, so the family made the move and their original home went back to the bank. It left a horrible stain on their credit that took years to clear off, but Courtney and her husband went on to buy that rental and make it their own.

A test can (and usually does) become a testimony, if you keep trusting God through it. He hasn't brought you this far to leave you hanging now! He's got big things ahead for you!

AFFIRMATION

With God's help, I can ace this test.

FAKERS

Difficulties and seasons of transition are
not designed to devastate you, but to ignite
the bigger dreams, life, love and abundance
you were destined for all along.

Marshawn Evans Daniels

Savannah was a terrific friend to Meg . . . except when she wasn't. Most of the time she was right there—at the birthday parties, the graduations, the baby showers, and everything in between. The first to arrive, the last to stay and help clean up, she proved her friendship over and over.

Or so Meg thought.

Every now and again Meg would hear from a mutual friend that Savannah had betrayed her trust by sharing deeply personal stories with others, stories that had been shared in complete confidence. When she confronted Savannah about this, she denied it, though the evidence proved otherwise.

After three separate incidences, Meg chose to step away. It took a lot of courage, but she couldn't handle the fakery, especially from someone who knew her deepest, darkest secrets. It didn't take long for Savannah to come to her, admitting what she'd done and asking for forgiveness. She forgave her, but it took some time before they grew close again.

No doubt you've been there. The betrayal hurts. Now you're wondering how to move forward.

Tomorrow is brighter, but only if you turn on the lights. You've got to illuminate the pain in order to deal with it. Otherwise it will lurk in the shadow and make a mess of things. It's not easy to confront someone who's betrayed you, but if you let them get away with it for long, they'll hurt others too.

While you're busy tending to these folks who've hurt you, don't forget to look at your own heart. Are you who you say you are? Have you ever betrayed a friend? Perhaps it's time for you to do a little apologizing of your own.

AFFIRMATION
I have discernment. I can tell the fakers from the true friends.

COURAGE TO KEEP STANDING

Courage is contagious. When a brave man takes a
stand, the spines of others are often stiffened.

Billy Graham

Have you ever had a "chronic" issue? Maybe
you had a nagging toothache that just
wouldn't go away. Or perhaps you struggled
with arthritis pain that could be considered
"chronic" because it gave you grief on a daily
basis.

Some people deal with autoimmune
diseases—diabetes, rheumatoid arthritis, or
Lupus, to name a few. Others are fighting a
battle against fibromyalgia or neurosensory
issues. These folks have come to know the word
chronic. They wish they didn't have ongoing
health issues, but the struggle is real.

So, what do you do if you're one of the
millions in chronic pain? How do you cope?
How does the desire to be pain free affect your
faith? Do you really stand a chance of things
getting better?

There's a wonderful story in the New
Testament about a woman who struggled
with a chronic illness. The Gospel of Matthew
calls her the woman "with an issue of blood"
(9:20 KJV), which tells us that she had chronic
hemorrhaging. When she heard that Jesus

was in town, she did the most daring thing imaginable. She worked her way through the crowd, maybe on her hands and feet, until she could finally reach the hem of His garment. The moment she touched Him, healing coursed through her body!

Jesus, feeling the healing power going forth, called out, "Who touched Me?" (Luke 8:45 KJV). Do you think He actually needed an answer? No, He already knew who had touched Him. But He wanted her to speak it, to make it real. He knew it would increase her faith. It also immediately changed the village's perception of her. No longer "unclean," she would now be welcomed back in society.

He wants you to make it real too. Today, lean in to Him. No matter how many times you've already prayed, pray again. Press your way through. Don't stop fighting. Whether your miracle comes through a divine touch (healing) or through a deeper relationship with Him through the pain, the safest place to be is touching Him.

AFFIRMATION

In this world I will have tribulation, but Jesus has overcome the world.

HOPE IS LIKE THE SUN,
WHICH, AS WE JOURNEY
TOWARD IT, CASTS
THE SHADOW OF OUR
BURDEN BEHIND US.

Samuel Smiles

TOMORROW'S FORECAST

You can't have a better tomorrow if you're
thinking about yesterday all of the time.

Charles Kettering

Remember that scene in *The Wizard of Oz* where Professor Marvel claims to see into the future? He leads Dorothy to believe that Auntie Em is going to mourn her loss if she goes away. Seeing into the future changes Dorothy's mind about running away. Once she sees what's going to happen, she turns around and goes back home, to the farm.

There are days when a crystal ball would come in handy, but God prefers we not know what's coming. (And, really . . . would you want to, if you knew that things were going to turn out differently than you'd hoped?)

No, it's better just to trust in Him and not try to predict the future. You can guess all day long, but knowing how things will work out? Well, that's only for the Lord to know.

Bonnie wished she had a crystal ball. After she and her husband applied for a mortgage, they waited . . . and waited . . . and waited. The days dragged on, minutes feeling like hours. Either the mortgage company was slow in responding or the news wasn't going to be good. She feared they wouldn't qualify. Or maybe they would. Yes, surely with their recent income increase, they were good candidates. Back and forth she went in her mind, trying to guess the future.

"Not knowing" was the hardest part of all. Bonnie nearly made herself sick in the days leading up to the news. Only when she got the "You're in!" call from her lender did she breathe a sigh of relief. Why did she fret? She should have just trusted God all along.

The Lord would prefer we not get ourselves worked up in a lather while we're waiting. The goal is to be at peace, even when we don't know the outcome. It's not easy, but when we learn to live like that, we're not knotted up in anxiety all the time.

One thing is for sure: God is in our tomorrows. We can't see Him, but He has already gone ahead of us. So, you can rest assured the future will be bright, because He's already there.

AFFIRMATION

I don't know what tomorrow holds, but I know who holds tomorrow.

THE COURAGE TO BE IMPERFECT

We don't have to allow failure to
prevent us from being used by God.*

Robert McGee

Mary Poppins claimed to be "practically perfect in every way." (Somewhat immodest, right?) Most folks these days feel the need to be perfect, just like Mary. Usually this starts when we're in our teens as we try to look like, dress like, and act like the others. It doesn't get much better after we marry or head into our occupations. We still fight the temptation to fit in by being like our peers, especially the perfect ones.

Oh, if only we looked that good in clothes!

If only our hair were fashionable like that.

If only we could go back to childhood and change one little thing.

If only we could find a better job.

If only we said the right thing at the right time like our practically perfect friend always did . . . and so on.

The comparison game becomes a daily struggle if we're not careful to guard our hearts.

This is especially true when we spend time on social media, where everyone puts their best foot (er, face) forward. If their posts are to be believed, our friends really are pictures of perfection, both on the job and at home. Wow! How did they get the golden ticket and all you got was the dog who drools on the furniture and the kids who leave their dirty socks on the floor?

Here's a fun fact: no one is perfect. Romans 3:10 (NIV) says, "There is no one righteous, not even one." So, all of those practically-perfect-in-every-way friends? They're not. Not even close.

Today, take the time to forgive yourself for the mistakes you've made. The flaws. The imperfections. The mess-ups. The mix-ups. Forgive yourself. And remember, there's only One who is perfect, and He thinks you're pretty amazing just as you are.

AFFIRMATION

Today I choose to do the hardest thing of all: forgive myself for not being perfect.

*Robert McGee, The Search for Significance: Seeing Your True Worth Through God's Eyes (Nashville: Thomas Nelson, 2003), 80.

MEMORY BANK DEPOSITS

Each day of our lives we make deposits in the
memory banks of our children.

Charles Swindoll

I have the best idea ever!" Deena said. "When
you turn thirteen, I'm going to take you to
Paris!"

"Really, Mom?" Nine-year-old Peyton let
out a squeal. "Ooh-la-la! I love Paris!"

"I know! It's all you ever talk about. Let's
start planning now, and when you're thirteen
we'll go, just you and me."

"Not Dad?"

"Nope." Deena shook her head. "This will
be a girls' trip, one we'll never forget. I'll start
planning now."

She set up a special account for the trip and
started putting money into it. Unfortunately,
after her divorce the money in that account had
to be used to pay for their move to a different house. And before she knew it, Peyton was
about to turn 13. There would be no trip to
Paris, but how could she tell her?

Deena was devastated and just knew Peyton
would be too. The nearly thirteen-year-old surprised her with, "I have an idea, Mom. Let's do
a Paris-themed party. I saw a picture online. It
will be easy and fun and not very expensive."

Deena hated that she had to add the "not very expensive" part but appreciated her daughter's thoughtfulness. Maybe one day they really would go to Paris. But for now, she would focus on planning the best Paris-themed birthday party any thirteen-year-old had ever had.

Maybe you've been there. You had grand ideas. Then the realities of your singleness kicked in and you realized you had to let that kiddo down. Again.

It's devastating not to be able to follow through, but sometimes you have no choice. When it comes to a choice between paying the rent or doing something fun with the kids, the rent comes first.

But that doesn't mean you can't plan fun experiences. Instead of going to Paris, France, go to Paris, Texas! (If you live in Texas, of course.) Instead of tickets to the big ball game, plan a ball-themed party at the house with cupcakes that look like baseballs.

You get the idea. You can make your kids' days bright, in spite of any circumstances you're walking through. Use your imagination and you'll come up with reasonably priced ideas in no time.

AFFIRMATION

I will make deposits into the memory banks of those I love on a regular basis!

HOPSCOTCHING ALONG

Life is not about how fast you run or how high
you climb but how well you bounce.

Vivian Komori

Remember playing hopscotch as a kid? You would start with a stellar chalk drawing on the driveway. Then you tossed a stone into a square and started hopping—only on one foot, unless the numbers lined up just right. Only then could you put that second foot down.

It's not always easy to keep your balance, especially if you're moving fast, but that's half the fun! You're testing your agility, after all.

The game of hopscotch dates back to thousands of years ago, when Roman soldiers would play with a purpose: to increase their speed and their amazing strength. Back in those days they would often hop over one hundred feet while carrying large weights. (Whew!)

Maybe you feel like those soldiers some days. You're loaded down with cares—hop, hop, hopping along, praying you can keep your balance. Are you getting enough sleep? Are you eating right? Do the kids have enough of your attention? Did you feed the dog? Did you pay the mortgage payment? Is there enough food in the pantry to cook a proper meal this evening? Do you need to go shopping? Would fast food (again!) be a problem?

Talk about a hopping (er, balancing) act!

Some days you just can't stay inside the lines, no matter how hard you try. You land far outside the safe boundaries. You end up yelling at the kids, fighting with your best friend, or getting irritated at your boss. (Hey, it happens!)

On days like that, remember to solidify your stance by spending time with the Lord. When you're out of balance, He's steady as a rock! And don't ever forget, the Holy Spirit isn't just your Comforter; He's also your guide. He'll keep you moving into many bright tomorrows if you keep your focus on Him and not on the agility course in front of you.

AFFIRMATION

Tomorrow will be better.
Until then, I'll lean on the Holy Spirit
and follow His lead.

WHEN THE BOUGH BREAKS

At sunset the little soul that had come with the dawning went away, leaving heartbreak behind it.

L. M. Montgomery

The world stopped spinning on the day Lynn got the news. She went in for a routine OB/Gyn visit to check on baby Evie's growth. Well into her fourth month, the baby girl should be growing like a weed.

The doctor put the scope on Lynn's belly but couldn't find Evie's heartbeat. After several failed attempts, Lynn was sent in for an ultrasound, where the horrifying news was confirmed.

Evie didn't make it.

Lynn fell apart at the seams. Everything she and her husband had dreamed of . . . planned for . . . gone. In an instant. The baby girl they had named, cherished, and joyously proclaimed as their own . . . no more.

After the sobbing stopped, all that was left was a sick, empty feeling, like nothing Lynn had ever experienced before. She wondered if the pain would ever leave or if she would feel like this forever.

Maybe you know Lynn's gut-wrenching pain all too well. You've been in her position. You've lost a child or a close loved one. And your world was rocked as never before. Shock. Disappointment. Grief. Emptiness. You felt it all. And, at the same time, you felt nothing. The sun kept shining, but you wished it wouldn't. People kept sending texts and cards, but you had nothing to say in response. And God? Where was He in the middle of this?

It's hard to picture "brighter days ahead" when you've lost everything. Seems impossible. And it's a cruel time for people to remind you that you'll "just get over it." You won't. Ever. But the Holy Spirit will—over a passage of time—ease the pain you're feeling and replace it with longing to see that precious face one day.

You will, you know. Your loved one will be waiting for you in heaven, where all the days ahead will be radiantly beautiful and you will spend them together.

AFFIRMATION

I can't wait to see my
loved one face-to-face.

IS THERE MORE?

Sometimes, the smallest things take
up the most room in your heart.

a. a. Milne

I don't know. I'm just feeling . . ." Dana paced
the room, trying to think of the right word.
"Discontent. I mean, I have a good life, but
there are days when I just feel like I'm going
through the motions. I work long hours, and
then I come home and cook and clean. I fall
into bed. Then I start all over again the next
day. Sometimes I wonder if it's all for nothing. I hardly have time to spend with Kevin or
the kids."

"I remember feeling that way when you were
little, Dana," her mother responded. "So, I
get it."

"What am I working for, anyway, if not to
give them a better life? How is being away from
them so much a better life?"

"Can I ask you a question, honey?" her mom
asked. "Do you feel like you had a good childhood?"

"Me?" Dana couldn't help but smile. "The
best! We lived in a great house in an awesome
school district. I loved our church and our
neighborhood. And remember those great road
trips we used to take? I loved all of that."

"Mm-hmm." Her mom paused. "Don't you see? I was working full-time just like you are now. But you're not remembering what you missed out on. You're only remembering the things Dad and I managed to pack into the hours when we were all together. So don't feel too bad about your schedule. God will show you how to prioritize to give the kids adequate time. They'll come away with great memories too."

Maybe you can relate to Dana's plight. It feels like your life is all work and no play, with little time left over for others. Perhaps it's time to put a plan in motion for an upcoming trip or a little vacation with your hubby or close friend. As you look toward the future with those you love, you'll be reminded that there is certainly more to your existence than work.

AFFIRMATION

I won't get hung up on how many hours I spend with my loved ones. I'll just make them the best hours possible!

YOUR WORTH IS IN HIM

Your value doesn't decrease based on
someone's inability to see your worth.

Anonymous

Rhonda flew under the radar much of her
life. There were plenty of other people
more talented, more boisterous, or more spiri-
tual. Whenever she compared herself to them,
she often wondered if she had anything to offer.

Rhonda wanted to play softball in high
school and did her best at tryouts but didn't get
picked for the team. When the choir director
asked her to audition for the spring show at
her school, she sang her favorite song but didn't
get picked. She ended up working in the tech
department backstage. Rhonda really enjoyed
the experience and did her best, though she got
no applause like the ones onstage.

When she got to college, Rhonda excelled
and ended up graduating at the top of her
class. She wasn't the sort to brag on herself,
and, strangely, no one else seemed to brag on
her, either. Her parents gave her a few pats on
the back but nothing more.

When she got married, Rhonda's husband
wasn't the kind who would gush over how
pretty she looked or how well she kept the
house, though she gave both her best shot. At

her workplace, she sold more insurance policies than her fellow employees, but her boss gave praise to others, not her. After a while, Rhonda wondered if others saw any worth in her at all.

Maybe you're a Rhonda. You're wondering, even now, why people seem to see right past you. They don't notice your talents or abilities.

Oh, but there is One who does notice, and He thinks you're the cat's meow! He planted those gifts and abilities inside of you and has been there all along, stirring them up. And He will place you in just the right place at the right time to use them.

Does it matter if you don't get the applause or accolades? Sure, it would be nice to have those things from time to time. But even if it doesn't come from those around you, just picture your heavenly Father clapping madly and saying, "You go, girl!"

AFFIRMATION

Today I ask for God's vision,
that I might see myself as He does—
a woman of many talents!

SCARS OR STARS

Being in Christ, it is safe to forget the past;
it is possible to be sure of the future; it is
possible to be diligent in the present.

Alexander MacLaren

Meredith was diagnosed with skin cancer when she was in her forties. The spot was awkwardly placed on her face, just to the left of her nose. The plastic surgeon decided that a small surgery would be necessary, one that would require nearly a dozen stitches.

Meredith was mortified. What would she look like afterward? Would the scar be prominent, or could she cover it with makeup once the site healed?

It took several weeks for the surgery site—close to two inches long—to heal and for a scar to form. Fortunately, the surgeon had done an excellent job with his stitches and the resulting scar wasn't terribly prominent after all. Still, it was the first thing she noticed whenever she glanced in the mirror. Was it the first thing others saw too?

Maybe you feel scarred like Meredith. Oh, the scars might not be on the outside, visible to a watching world. But you've been scarred by the pain you've experienced. The situations that hurt you the most have left their marks.

And you're worried those scars are visible to others.

It's time to change the way you think about those scars. Could you begin to see them as what they are. . .stars? They are, you know, for they are a reminder not of the pain but of the proof that you overcame that situation.

Meredith's doctor got all that cancer out when he performed surgery, and it never returned. She was able to relax and look forward to brighter days ahead because she didn't have that "What if?" hanging over her head.

You can relax too. You're an overcomer. And God is going to take the scars of yesterday and turn them into the stars of tomorrow if you trust Him to do so.

AFFIRMATION

May I never be so scarred
that I refuse to see the stars.

THEREFORE I TELL YOU, DO NOT WORRY ABOUT YOUR LIFE, WHAT YOU WILL EAT OR DRINK; OR ABOUT YOUR BODY, WHAT YOU WILL WEAR. IS NOT LIFE MORE THAN FOOD, AND THE BODY MORE THAN CLOTHES?

Matthew 6:25 NIV

ONE STEP AT A TIME

A hero is an ordinary individual who finds the strength to persevere and endure in spite of overwhelming obstacles.

Christopher Reeve

After an accident that broke her tibia and fibula, Jenny had to undergo surgery for the bones to be pinned and plated back together. She spent several days in the hospital and then another few days in a rehab hospital

Finally free to go home in a wheelchair, she faced an unexpected challenge. Jenny lived alone in a two-story townhome with her bedroom upstairs and the living area downstairs. She planned to spend her daytime hours downstairs so that she could let her two dogs in and out, but how would she get up to the second floor at night? And once she got there, how would she manage getting down the hallway to her room?

A plan came to her, one that just might work. She needed the help of a friend to implement it for the first time, but her friend was happy to oblige. Jenny rolled her wheelchair to the foot of the stairs and scooted out. She sat backward on the stairs and then—one at a time—eased her way up until she finally reached the top of the stairs. Once there, she managed to get into the rolling office chair her friend had strategically placed. Then she rolled across the wooden floor to her bedroom. Perfect! Worked like a charm.

We can get pretty creative when we have to, right? But, scooting up the stairs on your backside? That's not something you ever think you'll have to do.

There are situations, however, when you have no choice but to move one step at a time. The situation seems too overwhelming otherwise. You think to yourself, "There's just no way. I'll never make it through this."

One foot in front of the other, sister. Tomorrow is waiting with open arms but only if you take steps in that direction (even if they're small ones).

AFFIRMATION

I will take one step at a time.

THE COURAGE TO SHOW UP
(HEY, YOU SHOWED UP!)

Courage doesn't always roar. Sometimes
courage is the quiet voice at the end of the day
saying, "I will try again tomorrow."

Mary Anne Radmacher

Hey, you. Yes, you! The one who's been so hung up on the struggles that moving forward has been difficult. You've come a long way, baby! No, really. Think of how much braver you've gotten over the years. The things that used to frighten you? They're no big deal now. The things that used to keep you awake at night? You hardly think about them anymore. You're tougher now and better able to face the future without all the trembling.

Oh, I know—you don't see yourself that way, but you've made a lot of progress lately. You're stronger, braver, and kinder too. You've tackled financial matters, housing issues, relationship woes, and even job-related chaos, and you've come through like a champ. You showed up for the hard moments. You showed up for the heartbreaking moments. You showed up in the muck and mire of the daily grind, and you learned from every terrible, horrible, no-good, very bad day that you're capable of more than you ever knew.

Don't ever sell yourself short. With God on your side, you're a powerhouse! And when you're courageous, you're unstoppable!

So keep on showing up. And lead the way for children, friends, relatives, and fellow employees. People are looking to you. They're saying, "If she can do it, I can too."

So, do it.

Then keep doing it.

Then do it some more.

AFFIRMATION

Courage isn't something
I feel; it's something I do.

LIVE YOUR FAITH

Dear Friend,

This book was prayerfully crafted with you, the reader, in mind. Every word, every sentence, every page was thoughtfully written, designed, and packaged to encourage you—right where you are this very moment. At DaySpring, our vision is to see every person experience the life-changing message of God's love. So, as we worked through rough drafts, design changes, edits, and details, we prayed for you to deeply experience His unfailing love, indescribable peace, and pure joy. It is our sincere hope that through these Truth-filled pages your heart will be blessed, knowing that God cares about you—your desires and disappointments, your challenges and dreams.

He knows. He cares. He loves you unconditionally.

BLESSINGS!
THE DAYSPRING BOOK TEAM

Additional copies of this book and
other DaySpring titles can be purchased
at fine retailers everywhere.
Order online at <u>dayspring.com</u>
or
by phone at 1-877-751-4347